YOU ARE MINE & I AM YOURS

A WESLEYAN PRAYER FOR KIDS

Robert W. Lee
Melissa Collier Gepford

Illustrated by Kasia Jakubowska

• BARNSLEY INK •
RALEIGH, NORTH CAROLINA

• BARNSLEY INK •
RALEIGH, NORTH CAROLINA

For my son, Finnegan,
who asks the biggest and best questions
about God and sees the wonder in it all.

— *Melissa Collier Gepford*

For my mom, Sherrie,
who, like Susanna Wesley,
taught her children more of God
than all the theologians in the land.

— *Robert W. Lee*

"The best of all is, God is with us."
– John Wesley, 1791

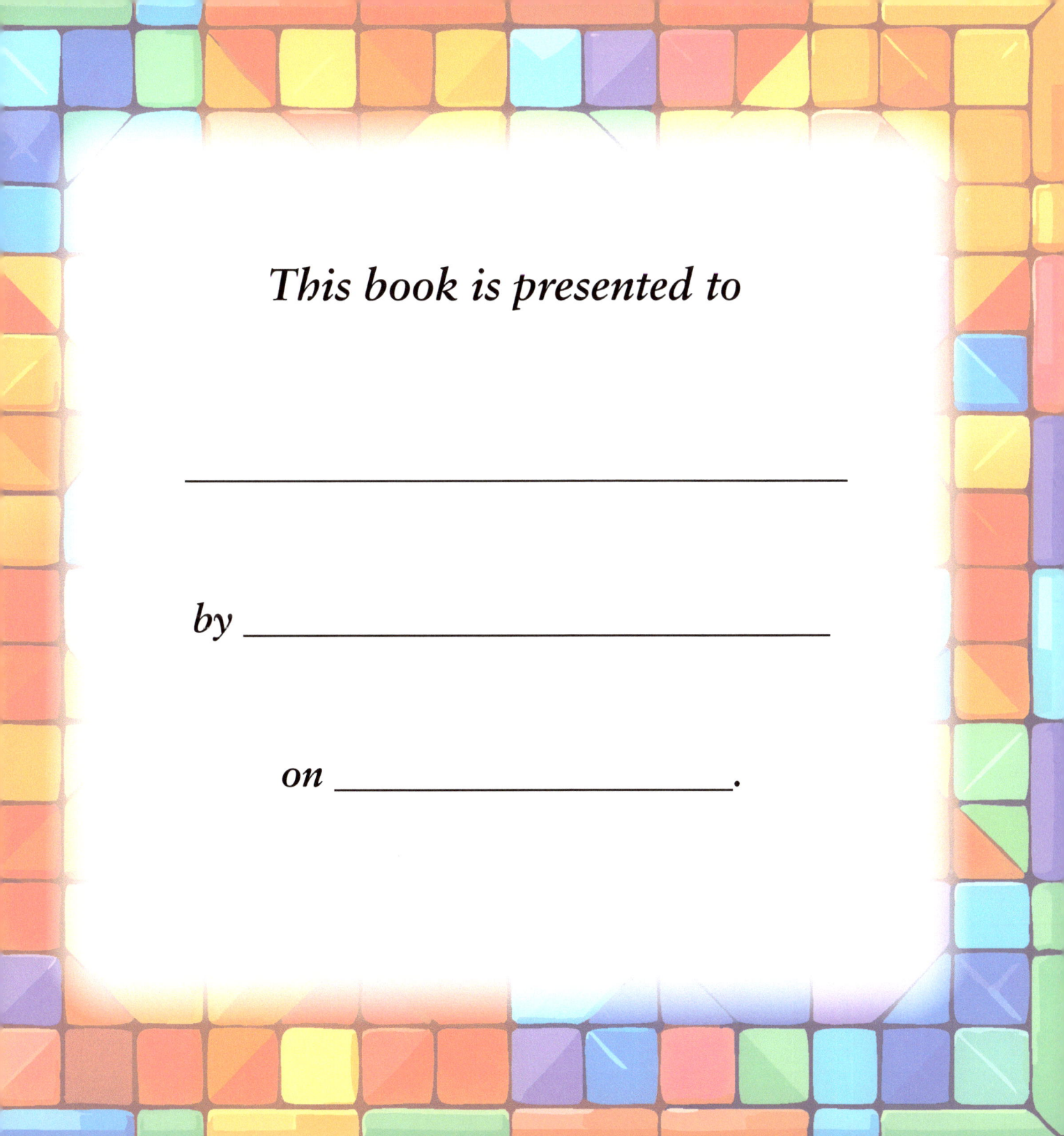

This book is presented to

_____

by _____

on _____.

An Introduction

The Covenant Prayer in the Wesleyan Tradition is a prayer that is part of a Covenant Renewal Service developed by John Wesley himself. Wesley was an Anglican clergyman and reformer in the 18th century. He lived from 1703-1791 in England. His life, writings, and witness gave birth to a movement that brought forth denominations like the United Methodist Church, the African Methodist Episcopal Church, and the Nazarene Church. His impact is still felt to this day well beyond the confines of those churches. Many of the denominations that he has inspired pray the covenant prayer at the beginning of the year as a means of renewal, but it is appropriate at all times of the year. The prayer has been used regularly in worship by Wesleyans in Britain dating back to 1755. Its truth is timeless and relevant still today.

Recognizing the prayer is written in 18th century language (you can read the original prayer and more about John Wesley in the back of this book), we attempted to encapsulate the prayer for modern, younger disciples of Jesus. In the spirit of John Wesley, we reformed the prayer while maintaining its original intent. We commend this work and pattern of life in the spirit and zeal of Mr. Wesley to your families that you may know the fullness of a living and loving God.

Melissa and Rob

God, I know it's not all about me,
but I know you hold me in your hand.

I trust you to take care of me
no matter what I do or who I'm with,

when things are easy or when things are hard,

when I am busy or when I'm bored,

when I'm winning or when I'm losing.

I trust you when I have a lot,
and I trust you when I have a little,

when I have everything
or when I have nothing.

With an open heart and open hands,
I give my life to you because I trust you
and you know me.

And now, dear loving God —
Parent, Child, and Spirit —

You are mine, and I am yours.
Forever and always.

May you hear my promise today with a glad heart all the way where you are. Amen.

For the Grown-Ups

Raising littles is such sacred work. Kissing a booboo, laughing wildly and freely at an inside joke, wiping tears from their face after a big disappointment—what a beautiful honor!

The Wesleyan Covenant Prayer wouldn't exist without John Wesley's mother, Susanna. She invested in each of her children in countless ways, physically, mentally, emotionally, and spiritually. Also known as the Mother of Methodism, Susanna spent countless hours instilling a love for God and neighbor into all her children, two of whom grew up to spark the Methodist Movement. *You Are Mine & I Am Yours* is just as much Susanna's legacy as Charles and John's.

Did you know there are many ways to connect with God? We invite you to try prayer practices that resonate with who your child is and what they love to do. Are they contemplative? Ask questions! Creative? Make something beautiful together! Higher energy? Get moving and play! Enjoy traditional forms of prayer? Lean into those! We hope the following ideas spark in you a love for engaging spiritually with the little ones in your life because, let's face it, children are the most wonder-full theologians!

Wonder

Wondering questions are meant to spark conversation. There is no right or wrong answer. Ask questions in such a way that feels less like an interrogation and more like you're curious to hear from your little one. You can model answering questions by remaining open and sharing your thoughts with them too!

- What does being safe feel like?

- Who do you trust most? How do you know you can trust them?

- Is it easier to trust God when things are easy or hard? Why?

- Do you feel closer to God when you are busy or when you are bored? Why?

- Do you feel more loved when you are winning or losing? Why?

- Is it easier to trust when you have a lot or a little? Why?

- How does it feel to say, "You are mine, and I am yours"?

Make

God made us in God's image - which means we're created to create! Gather your supplies, set up your space, and make something beautiful together. Here are a few ideas:

■ PRAYER JAR

You will need: a jar, pens, strips of paper to write on.

Set up a space in your home to place the jar, paper, and pens. Every day or once a week or just whenever (whatever works for your family), each family member is invited to write down or draw something they trust God with (e.g., "I trust God when I feel scared at night") on a slip of paper and put it in the jar. Over time, you will see how much you trust God and how God has been faithful.

◩ TRUST BRIDGE

You will need: household items (like straws, toothpicks, popsicle sticks, etc.), masking tape, small toy.

Invite the family to build a bridge or structure that can withstand the weight of a small toy. You may choose to use a timer. Large families may choose to work in two or more smaller groups. After the bridge holds the toy, invite a discussion about building trust. Trust supports us like the bridge. How can we know whom to trust? What does trust feel like? When can we trust God?

◪ FAMILY TRUST MAP

You will need: paper map OR computer or tablet.

Using a paper map or digital device with an age appropriate map app, pin places where each family member has experienced God or needed to trust God (e.g., school, hospital, park, sporting event). Invite everyone to share how they experienced God in those spaces.

Play

Play is a spiritual practice for all ages! We know that children learn through play. We grown-ups could all use a little more play in our lives too. So make some time to intentionally connect with your little ones in their own language—play!

EMOTION CHARADES

Invite your group to play charades with a twist. Taking turns, each person acts out an emotion without speaking. Others try to guess which emotion it is. After someone guesses correctly, discuss how that emotion feels in your body and how God is with us in that emotion, even if we don't feel like God is there.

FLOATING EXPERIMENT

You will need: large mixing bowl of water, heavy objects that sink and light objects that float

Conduct an experiment together. Let family members guess which objects will float and which will sink, then test it out. Objects that sink represent times when we feel heavy or weighed down, and objects that float represent times when we feel light or uplifted. The water represents God's love. It always surrounds us, whether we're floating or sinking! Bonus points if you have a sponge: that can represent how we can soak up God's love and share that love with others.

TRUST WALK

You will need: objects to create a safe obstacle course, blindfold

Build a safe obstacle course indoors or outdoors. Have one family member blindfolded while another guides them around the obstacle course using only their voice—no peeking! After everyone has a turn, discuss how you had to rely on each other when you couldn't see the path ahead. How does it feel to trust someone else for guidance? What does it look like and feel like to trust God?

Pray

John Wesley's Covenant Prayer is one of many prayers written down throughout history. Did you know there's no one right way to pray? There's breath prayer, movement prayer, meditation, coloring while praying, Daily Examen, reading the Psalms, the five finger prayer, the ACTS prayer, and the list goes on and on and on. We invite you to try out all sorts of methods together and see what resonates with you. Here are a few to try together:

■ BREATH PRAYER

A breath prayer is a quick, easy way to pray and find some peace in your busy day. It's a short prayer you repeat silently while you breathe. As you breathe in, you say the first part of the prayer in your mind, and as you breathe out, you say the second part. This helps you calm your mind and feel connected to God, no matter where you are or what you're doing. It's perfect for those hectic moments when you need a quick reset.

> Breathe in: "You are mine."
> Breathe out: "I am yours."

■ PRAYER CIRCLE

Sit in a circle and take turns lifting up prayers of thanksgiving/gratitude or asking for help from God. After each person shares, everyone says, "This is our prayer." This practice fosters community and feelings of support. If you've got silly little ones, invite them to say their prayer in a silly voice or very slowly, for dramatic effect.

■ PRAYER STRETCHES

If you need a little more movement in your prayer practice, add in some stretches or yoga poses as you pray together. Pray each line from this book while performing a sun salutation or your favorite stretches together. For example, while reaching arms up, say, "I trust you when I am busy." While folding forward, say, "I trust you when I am bored."

The Covenant Prayer

The Covenant Prayer in the Wesleyan Tradition can be found in the United Methodist Hymnal (Hymn No. 607) and in this book. This service was adapted and formed by John Wesley in the mid-1700's from Puritan Richard Alleine's 1663 volume. The first Methodist Covenant Renewal Service was held in 1755 at a church in London. Over 1,800 people were present and renewed their lives for the purposes of God.

Soon, such services would be held yearly at the beginning of the year to renew the vigor of Christians' service to the world and to the God who called the world into being. That said, it can be prayed in any context and at any point in the year. A newer, more modern prayer would later be adapted for use as the older language became increasingly archaic, yet it still missed the opportunity to connect with children. In 2024, the version in this book was written in the hopes of inspiring a new generation of followers of Jesus to follow in his footsteps, something that John Wesley did so well.

The Original Covenant Prayer in the Wesleyan Tradition

John Wesley

I am no longer my own, but thine.
Put me to what thou wilt, rank me with whom thou wilt.
Put me to doing, put me to suffering.
Let me be employed by thee or laid aside for thee,
exalted for thee or brought low for thee.
Let me be full, let me be empty.
Let me have all things, let me have nothing.
I freely and heartily yield all things
to thy pleasure and disposal.
And now, O glorious and blessed God,
Father, Son, and Holy Spirit,
thou art mine, and I am thine. So be it.
And the covenant which I have made on earth,
let it be ratified in heaven. Amen.

John Wesley

The Rev. John Wesley was a priest in the Church of England during the 1700s. He saw the Church's potential and wanted it to be the best it could be, even though the Church had trouble seeing the best in itself. John had a method for everything (That's where we get Methodists!), and he inspired many people in England and in Colonial America to follow God with compassion and grace in their hearts. Today, many Christians trace their religious heritage to John Wesley—and there are many Methodists in England, the United States, and beyond. He wrote the Covenant Prayer Service in which the Covenant Prayer was first prayed.

Charles Wesley

John Wesley couldn't do his work of reforming the Church alone! His younger brother Charles came alongside John and helped him praise God in countless ways. Charles wrote over 6,500 hymns during his lifetime. You've probably sung some of them. Think about if you've heard "Christ the Lord is Risen Today!" or "Love Divine, All Loves Excelling" or "Hark! The Herald Angels Sing." If any of those sound familiar, you've definitely heard a Charles Wesley hymn. Like any set of brothers, Charles and John worked hard together but sometimes didn't get along. Even still they loved each other despite their disagreements, and it made all the difference.

Susanna Wesley

Susanna Wesley was the youngest daughter of 25 children born to a Puritan pastor and his wife. She would grow up to have 19 children with her husband Samuel—including John and Charles Wesley. Susanna believed in education and worked hard to educate her children both in school subjects and in the works of the Church of England. She made sure her children had what they needed to love learning and know God well. John would later say he learned more about God from his mother than from all of the theology teachers in England. Susanna remains a lasting example of a parent who loved her children so dearly she thought it right of them to know a loving God.

About the Authors

The Rev. Melissa Collier Gepford

The Rev. Melissa Collier Gepford is the Intergenerational Discipleship Coordinator of the Great Plains Conference of the United Methodist Church, in which she helps congregations establish healthy kids and youth ministries. She grew up in East Texas and graduated from Perkins School of Theology. As an ordained United Methodist deacon, she connects church people to the world. Melissa is a writer, speaker, and most recently, the creator of www.dandelion-marketplace.com where caregivers and ministry leaders can find theologically rich curriculum and other resources. She enjoys drinking good coffee, working out, and testing her semi-green thumb. Melissa and her husband Bill enjoy dancing when they can and love playing with their son, Finnegan.

The Rev. Dr. Robert W. Lee

The Rev. Dr. Robert W. Lee is a pastor and public theologian. Dr. Lee is a graduate of Appalachian State University, Duke University, and Pacific School of Religion. He is the author of five books and has preached in churches and cathedrals across the world from Los Angeles to Paris. He has also served churches varying in size and location all across North Carolina.

Dr. Lee's work often intersects with the public square. In July of 2020 he testified before the United States Congress Subcommittee on Federal Lands, in 2021 he offered a prayer at the Inaugural Prayer Service for President Joe Biden and Vice President Kamala Harris. Rob has subsequently written devotionals for President and Dr. Biden. In 2024 he offered the invocation at the national 4th of July celebration held at the White House. Additionally he is recognized for his preaching and social witness as a member of the Morehouse College Board of Preachers.

He is married to Stephanie, and they are the proud parents of two daughters, Athena and Phoenix. They have two dogs, Maggie and Frank. In his spare time Rob is an avid autograph collector. Visit his other works at www.roblee4.com.

Other Books by Robert W. Lee

Stained-Glass Millennials

A Sin by Any Other Name: Reckoning with Racism and the Heritage of the South

The Pulpit and the Paper: A Pastor's Coming of Age in Newsprint

Fostering Hope: A Prayerbook for Foster and Adoptive Families

Night Owl Prayers: A Prayerbook

www.ingramcontent.com/pod-product-compliance
Lightning Source LLC
Chambersburg PA
CBHW041618120626
46551CB00003B/496